CONTEMPLATING THE SHROUD

The Sorrowful Mysteries

J. Kevin Burke
and
Theresa Karminski Burke

BOOKS & MEDIA

Boston

Cover photo: Giuliani

ISBN 0-8198-7002-1

Printed and published in the U.S.A. by Pauline Books & Media, 50 Saint Pauls Avenue, Boston, MA 02130-3491.

http://www.pauline.org

Pauline Books & Media is the publishing house of the Daughters of St. Paul, an international congregation of women religious serving the Church with the communications media.

1 2 3 4 5 6   04 03 02 01 00 99

CONTENTS

PREFACE

I Will Manifest My Divinity

The Shroud of Turin is an ancient burial cloth that mysteriously bears the image of the body it once enwrapped. Through its detailed image, this cloth clearly witnesses to the type of death this man endured. He was crucified, crowned with thorns and wounded in the right side of the chest area—facts amazingly similar to those presented in the Gospel accounts of Jesus of Nazareth.

Scientific investigation of this phenomenon began in 1898 when Secondo Pia first photographed the Shroud. Later, as Pia carefully developed the photograph, a striking, majestic-like face began to appear—one he believed to be the face of Christ. Secondo Pia had discovered that the image on the Shroud was a photographic negative.

Subsequent years of investigation ended for some in 1988 when the results of a Carbon-14 dating were publicized. International media reported that the radiocarbon dating (Carbon-14) had found the cloth to date between 1260 and 1390. Was the Shroud merely a "Medieval Forgery"? Case closed?

I remember receiving the news with disappointment. Still, the Shroud held so many unexplainable qualities that even science failed to explain. New discoveries in the fields of archaeology, computer imaging, organic chemistry, botany and physics continue to point to the possibility that the Shroud is authentic.

I concluded for myself that the Shroud was a kind of relic, perhaps of medieval origin, and left it at that...until 1992 when it made a direct impact on my life. Although I am inclined toward skepticism regarding mysterious phenomena, the inspiration for this "shroud rosary" came from a prayer experience during that same year.

One evening while at prayer, an unexpected image came to me. I was in a large room with a group of media persons, scientists and others who were present for an exhibition of the Shroud of Turin. While everyone's attention was fixed on the image, it began to radiate a blinding light, and this light filled me with a presence I immediately sensed to be that of Jesus Christ. My first reaction was to withdraw from the experience, but the strong sense of Jesus' loving presence filled me with such peace, I continued to pray. Then Jesus spoke words that still resound within me: "I will manifest my divinity." The image faded, but that powerful sense of the divine remains impressed on my heart and mind.

I considered this remarkable experience a private inspiration to strengthen my own faith, so I shared it only with my wife, a close friend, and a relative whose discernment I trusted.

In 1995, I felt a strong desire to once again research the Shroud. I read *The Cross and The Shroud* written by Frederick T. Zugibe, Ph.D., M.D., an internationally renowned forensic scientist. I was impressed with his exhaustive study of the crucifixion and the Shroud of Turin, so much so that the book became instrumental in the development of the "shroud rosary." *The Cross and The Shroud* affirms the incredible sufferings of Christ's redemptive passion and death—and the true depth of his love for humanity.

Recent information regarding the Shroud of Turin appeared in a supplement to the March 1995 issue of *Inside the Vatican*. Here are just a few of the findings:

* The Shroud was rescued from a fire in 1532. The effects of the fire itself, the silver casing that housed the cloth and other factors have proved to corrupt a Carbon-14 dating by as much as 1,000 years or more.

* The wound marks on the Shroud are deposits of human blood, proven to be that of a male.

* The Shroud image is not a painting. The origin of the formation of the cloth's image remains a mystery.

(For further information see the appendix.)

This information inspired me with a greater appreciation of my own prayer experience, and encouraged me to contemplate the mystery of the Shroud. Dr. Zugibe's account of the sufferings and crucifixion of Jesus entered my reflection on the sorrowful mysteries of the rosary, which grew more fervent and spiritually fruitful. Each Hail Mary became a link in the chain binding me to Jesus as I prayerfully accompanied him on his agonizing journey to Calvary. It is my hope to share with you something of my experience through this "shroud rosary" of the sorrowful mysteries—concluding with the glorious mystery of the resurrection.

May the Holy Spirit unite your heart with the hearts of Jesus and Mary as you accompany him in his sufferings and experience the joy and wonder of his glorious resurrection.

INTRODUCTION

"Then he took bread, blessed it, broke it, and gave it to them, saying, 'This is my body which is given for you—do this in my remembrance.' Likewise he took the cup after they had eaten and said, 'This cup is the new covenant in my blood which is poured out for you'" (Lk 22:19–20).

Human relationships are more firmly joined through shared sufferings and joys. The purpose of these meditations is to help the pray-er to form a deeper union with the Sacred Heart of Jesus, to come to a fuller understanding of his great love for every human person, and to penetrate the profound meaning in his words: This is my body, which is given for you.

The "shroud rosary" is based on selections from the gospel accounts with reflections that use imaginative details. These are meant to help the pray-er develop mental images of the scenes described. Each mystery offers insights into the sufferings of Christ as illustrated by the Shroud of Turin, followed by a meditation-experience to help relive with Jesus, his walk to Calvary. Allow the words of the Hail Mary to focus your attention on this walk with Jesus and invite Mary to lead you to the loving heart of her Son.

Speak to Jesus about any difficulty, suffering, shame, guilt, or sin that may burden you. Offer prayers for those who cannot pray, those who need the love and saving power of Jesus Christ to enter their lives, those who suffer…. I have found the "shroud rosary" to be an even more vital prayer experience when accompanied by fasting, participation at the Eucharistic celebration and reception of Holy Communion.

May the Lord bless you and strengthen you on your journey.

THE SHROUD ROSARY

The Creed

I believe in God, the Father Almighty, Creator of heaven and earth. I believe in Jesus Christ, his only Son our Lord. He was conceived by the power of the Holy Spirit and born of the Virgin Mary. He suffered under Pontius Pilate, was crucified, died, and was buried. He descended to the dead. On the third day he arose again. He ascended into heaven, and sits at the right hand of the Father. He will come again to judge the living and the dead.

I believe in the Holy Spirit, the holy catholic Church, the communion of saints, the forgiveness of sins, the resurrection of the body, and life everlasting. Amen.

Father, I begin this rosary praising you, my Creator, and accepting your kingship over me.

Our Father

Our Father who art in heaven, hallowed be thy name. Thy kingdom come. Thy will be done on earth as it is in heaven.

Give us this day our daily bread, and forgive us our trespasses, as we forgive those who trespass against us. And lead us not into temptation, but deliver us from evil. Amen.

Mary, guide me as I enter into the mystery of Christ's saving love for me.

Hail Mary

Hail Mary full of grace, the Lord is with you. Blessed are you among women and blessed is the fruit of your womb, Jesus.

Holy Mary, mother of God, pray for us sinners, now and at the hour of our death. Amen.

With each bead, draw me closer to the heart of Jesus.

Hail Mary...

With each bead, draw me closer to your heart so that I may enter into the mystery of the suffering and death of your beloved son, Jesus.

Hail Mary...

Glory Be

Glory to the Father, and to the Son, and to the Holy Spirit, as it was in the beginning, is now and will be forever. Amen.

The Shroud Rosary Alternative Prayer:

An alternative in praying the "shroud rosary" could include substituting the following phrase in place of each Hail Mary:

> *Mary, draw me closer to the heart of your beloved son, Jesus.*

THE FIRST
SORROWFUL MYSTERY

The Agony in the Garden

Jesus, burdened with the knowledge that his suffering and death are now approaching, accepts the weight of humanity's sins and the abandonment of his closest followers. This anguish described by Luke, the disciple and physician, caused Jesus to sweat drops of blood (cf. Lk 22:44)—an extraordinary phenomenon called *hemathidrosis* which occurs when the blood vessels surrounding the sweat glands rupture, leaving the flesh painfully sensitive.

> *"When they came to a place named Gethsemane he said to his disciples, 'Sit here while I pray.' He took Peter and James and John along with him and he became very distressed and troubled, and*

he said to them, 'My soul is greatly distressed, to the point of death; stay here and keep watch'" (Mk 14:32–34).

"In his anguish he prayed more earnestly, and his sweat became like drops of blood falling to the ground" (Lk 22:44).

Our Father...

Hail Mary...

Clouds cover the full moon casting shadows across the ground. In the darkness ahead is the Mount of Olives. With determination you make your way toward the darkened ridge with a longing to become a follower of Jesus. Tonight you will ask him to accept you.

Hail Mary...

In the Garden of Gethsemane the disciples are huddled together against the night air. Peter looks wearied; the apostles James and John signal for you to join them. Jesus is resting against a large tree. He appears as one who carries the weight of great distress.

Hail Mary...

As you join the disciples you quietly explain, "I heard the Master preaching in the temple and his words of truth touched my heart." The others nod with understanding, accepting your presence, and you experience a sense of relief.

Hail Mary...

Glancing toward the group, Jesus' gaze settles on you with a look that touches your soul. Although exhausted those eyes retain the light which first drew you, but now you also see a fear and anxiety there. You too begin to feel anxious.

Hail Mary...

Jesus asks his disciples to remain awake and pray. "Pray that you won't be put to the test..." (Lk 22:40) He turns and walks away slowly. The disciples are somber and silent as they watch him disappear into the shadows.

Hail Mary...

Kneeling in prayer, Jesus rests his head in his hands. Then, lifting his face upward, his eyes widen with distress and his breathing becomes more rapid. He cries aloud, "My soul is greatly distressed, to the point of death..." (Mk 14:34). Your heart is only capable of sharing a small portion of what Jesus is experiencing—the dread, the anxiety, the struggle with his desire to have this cup of suffering pass him by. Your mind races: *he must flee; he isn't safe here in Jerusalem!*

Hail Mary...

As you turn to the disciples for help to per-
suade Jesus to leave, you find them sleeping
soundly, overcome with emotional fatigue. And
Jesus continues to pray alone. Once again his an-
guished voice breaks the stillness, "My Father, if
it's possible, let this cup pass away from me" (Mt
26:39). Moments pass in an agonizing silence.
The words that follow are resolute and clear, "My
Father, if it isn't possible for this cup to pass by
without me drinking it, let your will be done" (Lk
22:42).

Hail Mary...

All the sins of the past, present and future
generations weigh upon Jesus. The emotional
pain is so intense it causes him to sweat blood.
You humbly ask Jesus to forgive you for any resis-
tance in accepting God's will in your own life.

Hail Mary...

The sky begins to clear and the moon shines
down upon the solitary figure of Christ. Having
freely embraced his Father's will, Jesus continues
the night in prayer.

Hail Mary...

From the darkness, a crowd of temple guards

enters the garden, with Judas leading the way. He approaches Jesus, embraces him, greeting him with a kiss. One of his own disciples hands the Son of Man over to death—the pain of this betrayal is reflected in Jesus' eyes.

Glory and honor to you, Lord Jesus Christ. I love you and praise you my Savior. Thank you for accepting this pain and humiliation. Strengthen my belief in your great love for me and for all people.

Glory to the Father...

THE SECOND SORROWFUL MYSTERY

The Scourging at the Pillar

The Roman *flagrum* was an ancient penal instrument used in the scourging of criminals. This whip of leather thongs had small pieces of metal or bone attached to the end of each strip. The scars covering the body on the Shroud of Turin indicate that the lashes received numbered between 100 and 120, extending across the shoulders, back, chest and legs.

"'He did no wrong, and no deceit was found on his lips.' When he was reviled he didn't reply in kind,

when he suffered he made no threats; instead, he entrusted himself to the One Who judges justly. It was he who bore our sins in his body on the cross so that we could die to sin and live in righteousness; by his wounds you've been healed" (1 Pt 22:24).

Our Father...

Hail Mary...

With an early morning mist still in the air, you stand waiting for some sign of Jesus. Finally Jesus is led outside to the courtyard of the Roman procurator where he will suffer the humiliation of being stripped of his clothing.

Hail Mary...

The soldier seizes Jesus by the arm and shoves him toward a pillar. His arms are stretched above his head while a soldier binds his hands to the column. His body trembles with the anticipation of this cruel ordeal.

Hail Mary...

Another soldier steps forward, gripping a *flagrum*, his muscular arms revealing a capacity for brutal power. He draws the *flagrum* back and puts the force of his strength into the first blow. You hear the sharp sound of the *flagrum* as it whips through the air and encounters human flesh. You cover your eyes in horror.

Hail Mary...

With every strike the leather thongs and metal pieces slice deep wounds into Jesus' flesh. Your anguish increases as the scourging continues and Jesus' blood falls to the ground.

Hail Mary...

No part of the Lord's sacred body is spared. Under the soldier's cutting blows, Jesus shudders in agony; his flesh covered with gaping wounds.

Hail Mary...

The incessant beating continues and you pray that each blow will be the last. You stand by helplessly as Jesus' head falls back in pain.

Hail Mary...

You tremble with sorrow at the sight of his sacred body ravaged by so many wounds. Jesus, no longer capable of supporting himself under the blows, hangs limply from the pillar.

Hail Mary...

Finally the soldier stops. Your heart is overcome with grief as you see your Lord covered with countless open wounds.

Hail Mary...

Except for his labored breathing, Jesus is motionless. Then, as he is released from the pillar, he collapses to the ground. All at once you are aware that Jesus has suffered all of this because of his great love for you.

Hail Mary...

You sense the spiritual nearness of Mary and her invitation to join her in adoring her son. Your heart reaches out to offer Jesus some comfort and to thank him.

Glory and honor to you, Lord Jesus Christ. I love you and praise you my Savior. Thank you for accepting this pain and humiliation. Strengthen my belief in your great love for me and for all people.

Glory to the Father...

THE THIRD SORROWFUL MYSTERY

The Crowning with Thorns

The head of the man on the Shroud bears deep puncture wounds—reminiscent of the crowning of Jesus with thorns as described in the Gospel accounts. Unlike many artistic depictions however, the Shroud shows that the crown of thorns covered the entire head, like a cap. According to Dr. Zugibe in *The Cross and The Shroud*, the crown of thorns was a major source of suffering. By forcing the thorns onto the cranium, with its nerve endings close to the skin, an excruciating pain erupted over the entire facial region and ears. Thereafter, the slightest pressure to this injured region would renew the unspeakable pain, and the Shroud clearly indicates severe bruising and swelling resulting from repeated blows to the face. The suffering of the crown of thorns accompanied Jesus throughout his passion.

> "So the soldiers led him away inside the courtyard, that is, the praetorium, and called the whole cohort together. They dressed him in a purple robe and put on him a crown they had woven from thorns, and they began to greet him, 'Hail, King of the Jews!' Then they'd hit his head with a reed, and spit on him and kneel and worship him. And when they had mocked him they stripped the purple robe off him, dressed him in his own clothes, and led him out..." (Mk 15:16–20).

Our Father...

Hail Mary...

The sun sends its rays through the fading mist, warming the cold stone walls surrounding the governor's palace. Jesus, trembling with pain and weakness after the brutal scourging, faces the soldiers.

Hail Mary...

Still dazed by the physical trauma, Jesus can hardly remain standing before the soldiers. As he lifts his head to look at them, his eyes are filled with compassion despite his own suffering.

Hail Mary...

Pulling off branches from a nearby thorn bush, one of the soldiers weaves a cap. Cursing when one of the large barbs stabs his thumb, he throws it to the ground and then cautiously picks it up again.

Hail Mary...

As he finishes making this crown of mockery, the soldier grins, lifts it into the air, and proclaims sarcastically, "A royal crown for the King of the Jews!" His cohorts roar with laughter and join him in the ridicule.

Hail Mary...

A soldier forces the crown onto Jesus' head and the twisted branches, with their large thorns, pierce his flesh. Blood trickles down his face and neck. "Long live the King of the Jews!" Laboring under the pain Jesus breathes deeply and lowers his eyes, freely accepting even these insults for our salvation.

Hail Mary...

Carrying a purple robe, a soldier approaches Jesus and pretends to offer him reverence, bowing low and draping the royal robe over Jesus' shoulders. The soldiers laugh in contempt, taking pleasure in this taunt.

Hail Mary...

Other soldiers pay false homage by bringing a large stick to the "King of the Jews" and placing it, like a royal scepter, into Jesus' hands. Then seizing the stick, a soldier strikes Jesus on the head while others slap his face. Each time the soldier strikes Jesus' head, the thorns penetrate deeper. This cruelty and ceaseless derision fills you with indignation.

Hail Mary...

The blows to his head send waves of burning pain across Jesus' face and he stiffens his body to brace himself against the beating. The soldiers permit Jesus no respite from the torment.

Hail Mary...

They salute Jesus with slaps to his face and

you watch helplessly. Blood continues to stream down his bruised and swollen face and you cannot imagine how much more Jesus will have to suffer for the salvation of every human person.

Hail Mary...

At the sight of Jesus' suffering, you are over-come with sorrow for your own sins. He is offer-ing his life freely for the forgiveness of sins—your own and those of all people, in every time. Once again you sense Mary's presence strengthening you as you bow before the Lord, trusting in his merciful love.

Glory and honor to you, Lord Jesus Christ. I love you and praise you my Savior. Thank you for ac-cepting this pain and humiliation. Strengthen my belief in your great love for me and for all people.

Glory to the Father...

THE FOURTH
SORROWFUL MYSTERY

The Carrying of the Cross

According to the practice of Roman crucifix-ion, the condemned was forced to carry the crossbeam on his shoulders. The vertical beam, already fixed outside the city walls at the sight of the crucifixion, awaited him. This upper cross-beam might weigh anywhere from 50 to 100 pounds. As the victim struggled toward the place of execution, he was subjected to the abuse and jeering of the executioners and bystanders.

The Shroud testifies to this prelude—a horrific form of execution. The image shows an upper back area covered with large abrasions. Along with these injuries, others are observable: the seriously damaged left knee, the sides of the face, the broken nose, the forehead—all of which indicate a number of falls. These details are consistent with the Gospel accounts of Jesus' painful way to crucifixion; the half mile course to Golgotha began around noon.

> "Pilate…led Jesus outside and sat on the judgment seat at the place called 'the Pavement,' but in Hebrew, 'Gabbatha.' Now it was the Day of Preparation for the Passover; it was about noon. And he said to the Jews, 'Here is your king!' They shouted, 'Away with him, away with him! Crucify him!' Pilate said to them, 'Shall I crucify your king?' The chief priests answered, 'We have no king but Caesar!' Then he handed him over to them to be crucified" (Jn 19:13–16).
> "As they were leading him away they seized

Simon, a Cyrenean, who was coming from the country, and laid the cross on him to carry behind Jesus. Now a large crowd of the people was following him, as well as women who were lamenting and wailing for him" (Lk 23:26–27).

Our Father...

Hail Mary...

Surrounded by a crowd that demanded Jesus' crucifixion, you watch as Pontius Pilate declares, "I'm innocent of this man's blood." Vehement shouts erupt from the crowd, "To the cross with him! Crucify him! Crucify him!"

Hail Mary...

The news of the sentence spreads quickly. People hasten to the street where the condemned Jesus will pass. Only a short time ago many in the crowd had hailed Jesus as messiah; now, upon seeing him pass by, they wear the many human faces of disappointment, compassion, anger, distress, hatred....

Hail Mary...

Placing the heavy beam across Jesus' shoulders, the soldiers secure it to his arms. Jesus gasps in agony as the weight of the wooden beam intensifies the pain of the wounds left by the scourging.

Hail Mary...

The sun-baked street is like an oven fire as Jesus makes his way through the crowd. He struggles up the narrow street under the weight of the crossbeam, unable to maintain his balance as he walks on the uneven stones.

Hail Mary...

Physical and emotional sufferings have taken their toll on Jesus. Weakened by the copious loss of blood, he falls to the pavement. Because his arms are bound he cannot break his fall and his head hits the road under the force of the crossbeam's weight. Although wracked with pain, Jesus labors to rise to his feet.

Hail Mary...

Jesus makes his way, moving closer to where you are standing. He falls again and a cry of anguish escapes from the collapsed figure. You want to rush through the crowd to help him, but are paralyzed by fear of the soldiers. Jesus slowly struggles to his feet and continues forward with halting steps.

Hail Mary...

Some people in the crowd shout at Jesus, others lament the pitiful scene loudly. Growing weaker with every step, Jesus continues on toward Calvary. But once again, he collapses on the stone pavement.

Hail Mary...

Seeing that Jesus can no longer carry the crossbeam, a soldier scans the crowd for someone to take it the rest of the way. His eyes focus on you and you quickly look away. He singles you out of the crowd and commands you to take the crossbeam from Jesus. Out of fear you hurry to obey the order and carry the wooden burden on your own shoulders.

Hail Mary...

The weight of the crossbeam cuts into your shoulders and you are amazed that Jesus has carried it this far. As he walks beside you Jesus looks into your eyes. It is then that you grasp the meaning of human suffering as a unique opportunity to share in the suffering of Jesus.

Hail Mary...

Mary has accompanied Jesus during his way of suffering. Seeing her now, you want to urge her to leave this horrible scene. But in her tear-filled eyes there is a courage befitting the Mother of Sorrows. You ask Mary to help you find the courage and faith needed to follow Jesus to the end.

Glory and honor to you, Lord Jesus Christ. I love you and praise you my Savior. Thank you for accepting this pain and humiliation. Strengthen my belief in your great love for me and for all people.

Glory to the Father...

THE FIFTH SORROWFUL MYSTERY

The Crucifixion

The figure on the Shroud of Turin bears wounds corresponding with those described in the Gospel account of Jesus' crucifixion. There are large puncture wounds located on the wrist and feet and one in the right chest area. "One of the soldiers stabbed him in the side with a spear, and at once blood and water came out" (Jn 19:34). In one of the post-resurrection accounts Jesus invites Thomas to probe the nail marks in his hands and the wound in his side (cf. Jn 20:27).

In a crucifixion, the hands of the condemned were affixed to the upper cross beam with nails (often iron spikes about seven inches long) driven through the flesh just under the wrist, in the muscular area below the thumb. The condemned was then placed on the vertical portion of the cross and, once suspended, his feet were secured one over the other, by another nail.

"My God, My God, why have you forsaken me?
So aloof are you from my salvation!
Such are the words of my cry.

"It was in you that our fathers trusted.
They trusted, and you delivered them.
To you they lamented, and they escaped.
In you they trusted, and were not disappointed.
I, instead, am a worm not a man;
the shame of the human race, a disgrace to the
    nation.
All who see me hold me in derision;
they gape with their lips and shake their heads:
'Let him turn to Yahweh! Let him deliver him,
let him save him! For he is pleased with him.'

"Like water I am drained,
my bones are all disjointed;
my heart has become like wax,
melted as it is at the center of my being.
For dogs have surrounded me,
a gang of scoundrels have encompassed me;
like a lion, they are at my hands and feet.
I can count all my bones.
As for them, they look intently, they stare at me.
They divide my garments among themselves,
but for my tunic they cast lots" (Ps 22:2, 5–9, 15–19).

Our Father...

Hail Mary...

Reaching Calvary at last, his body bruised and broken, the Lord must still face the dreadful torture of crucifixion.

Hail Mary...

His garments, stained with blood and clinging to his body, are stripped off by the soldiers. Jesus groans in agony as his wounds are reopened. The soldiers take the large square nails and approach Jesus.

Hail Mary...

They position his arms, stretching them out on the crossbeam. Two soldiers hold his arms down while a third drives the nails into his wrists.

Hail Mary...

The sight of Mary dispels your urge to run from the terrible scene. She who had borne and nurtured Jesus, now witnesses his passion. Her heart, pierced by the suffering of her beloved son, remains steadfast even before the cross. You too remain at the cross to comfort Mary and to be comforted by her.

Hail Mary...

The soldiers lift the crossbeam and fasten it to the vertical beam. Jesus hangs in agony while his legs are positioned and a nail is driven into his feet. The sound of the hammer striking the iron nail causes you to shudder. You cannot bear to look at Jesus suspended there on the cross. Amid all of his incredible suffering, Jesus prays: "Father forgive them, for they don't know what they're doing" (Lk 23:34).

Hail Mary...

It is difficult for you to endure the sight of his ceaseless agony. The position of Jesus' body on the cross forces him to lift himself in order to breathe. This only intensifies the pain in his hands and feet. His love for you is greater than all his physical sufferings.

Hail Mary...

Adding to these physical sufferings, Jesus now experiences the abyss of abandonment and utter loneliness. He cries out in a loud voice, "My God, My God, why have you abandoned me?" (Mk 15:34). Mary stands near the cross weeping. Her son will accept every suffering for our salvation.

Hail Mary...

An ominous darkness moves over the land.

You see Jesus looking at Mary—such profound love and tenderness flows between them. She is supported by the apostle John. Jesus addresses Mary, "There is your son"; then to John, "She is your mother." You understand that the apostle John is now entrusted with the care of Mary. But there is much more to this tender gesture. Jesus is giving his mother to you and to all humanity.

Hail Mary...

Jesus cries out, "I am thirsty." A sponge soaked with bitter wine is lifted to his parched lips and Jesus tastes the drink. A heavy silence presses over those who still stand on Calvary under the darkening sky. Then, with his last breath, Jesus cries out, "Father, into your hands I entrust my spirit!" (Lk 23:46). And bowing his head, Jesus dies.

Hail Mary...

The darkness engulfing the hill of Calvary is broken by flashes of lightening. Along with the few who remain, you also linger before the cross with Mary. A soldier thrusts his spear into Jesus' side and blood and water flow from the heart of your Savior. Prostrate before the cross, you pray:

Glory and honor to you, Lord Jesus Christ. I love you and praise you my Savior. Thank you for ac-

cepting this pain and humiliation. Strengthen my belief in your great love for me and for all people.

Love and honor to you Mary, blessed daughter of the Father, Mother of our Redeemer and spouse of the Holy Spirit.

Glory to the Father...

THE GLORIOUS MYSTERY OF THE RESURRECTION

How the image on the Shroud was formed continues to be a mystery to science. French biophysicist and researcher in the area of nuclear medicine, Jean Baptiste Rinaudo, theorizes that the image was created by a radiation of protons emitted by the body itself under the effect of some "unknown source of energy" (*Inside the Vatican*, Turin Supplement VIII).

"On the first day of the week Mary Magdalene came to the tomb in the early morning while it was still dark, and she saw the stone, which had been taken away from the tomb. So she ran and came to Simon Peter and to the other disciple whom Jesus loved, and she said to them, 'They've taken the Lord out of the tomb and we don't know where they've put him!'

"So Peter and the other disciple went out and they went to the tomb. The two of them were running together, but the other disciple ran faster than Peter and came to the tomb first, and when he bent down he saw the linen cloths lying there, but he didn't go in. Simon Peter came, too, following him, and he went into the tomb and saw the linen cloths lying there, and the face covering, which had been on his head, wasn't lying with the linen cloths but was wrapped up separately in its own place" (Jn 20:1–7).

Our Father...

Hail Mary...

The drama of Calvary fades into a dream as you fall into an exhausted sleep near the entombed body of Jesus. The odors of moist earth and strong spices mingle in the damp air. You awaken in absolute darkness and remember that Jesus is dead, that his body is now wrapped in a linen shroud.

Hail Mary...

There is no sound in the heavy air of the tomb. Alone in the darkness and devastated with thoughts of Jesus' death, you struggle with your doubts. You want to believe his promise, but he is gone.

Hail Mary...

The darkness penetrates your soul, now overcome with fear, anxiety and doubt. You close your eyes and in your heart you ask Mary to help you to have a deeper faith in the redemptive love of Jesus.

Hail Mary...

An imperceptible sweetness begins to fill the air. The beautiful aroma grows more distinct, but the fragrance is unique and unfamiliar. At the same time you notice the atmosphere in the cave is becoming warmer, drier. Your eyes are drawn to a light near Jesus' body.

Hail Mary...

The faint light takes on an overwhelming intensity. It flashes, then bursts into streams of brilliant color, illuminating the interior of the tomb.

Hail Mary...

The ground trembles beneath you, forcing the large stone away from the entrance of the tomb. The tremors awaken the soldiers who run in fright and abandon their station outside the tomb.

Hail Mary...

All is silent. Confused by your own fear and anticipation, you peer outside from the entrance of the tomb. The sun's first rays are reaching over the horizon, and in the distance you see Calvary with the silhouette of the cross standing against the dawn.

Hail Mary...

Glancing back into the tomb, you become alarmed. The body is gone! Only the burial linens remain on the rock, undisturbed. Stunned, you rush to the opening of the tomb. Then you see him!

Hail Mary...

Outside the tomb the radiance of the resurrected, glorified Jesus envelops you. Brilliant light streams from the wounds in his hands, feet and side. Your entire being is flooded with inexpressible joy and peace; your heart, bursting with love and gratitude, sings praise to the Risen Savior. Jesus is risen from the dead! Alleluia, alleluia! Christ has conquered death and opened the way to eternal life! Alleluia, alleluia!

Hail Mary...

He *is* risen! Jesus speaks lovingly to your heart, "Peace be with you." All heaven and earth rejoice and the very air you breathe proclaims his holy presence. You kneel before him and proclaim:

Praise to you Lord Jesus Christ, King of endless glory. I love you and honor you, my Risen Savior!

Love and honor to you Mary, blessed daughter of the Father, Mother of our Redeemer and spouse of the Holy Spirit.

Glory to the Father...

"Let us give thanks to the God and Father of our Lord Jesus Christ who in his great mercy has given us new life through the resurrection of Jesus Christ from the dead. With living hope we look forward to possessing the rich inheritance prepared for us by God" (cf. 1 Pt 1:3–4).

APPENDIX

For the latest in scientific research, books, videos and a newsletter on the Shroud of Turin contact:

Turin Shroud Center
P.O. Box 25326
Colorado Springs, Colorado 80918
(719) 593-9613

The Internet has several sites with articles and information on the Shroud, as well as photos and other links. Some of the addresses are:

http://www.shroud.com
http://www.everlasting.org/shroud.htm
http://dmi-www.mc.duke.edu/shroud/findings.htm

The following readings on the Shroud of Turin are informative and inspiring:

Barbet, Pierre, M.D. *A Doctor at Calvary*. New York: T. J. Kennedy, 1953.

By analyzing the shroud of Turin, Dr. Barbet offers a powerful and detailed account of the passion of Jesus.

Gelles, Walter. "The Shroud Controversy Goes On." *Catholic Digest*, November 1990, 72–78.

Experts challenge the results of the C-14 dating of 1988. The opinions of respected scientists are presented, revealing major flaws in the testing.

"The Shroud of Turin." *Inside The Vatican*, March 1995, 22–41.

An excellent resource for a concise informative treatment of the Shroud with updated material from the fields of science and history.

Zugibe, Frederick T., Ph.D., M.D. *The Cross and the Shroud: A Medical Examiner Investigates the Crucifixion.* Garnerville, N.Y.: Angelus Books, 1982.

"A vivid definite picture of 7Christ's physical and mental suffering from the perspective of forensic medicine." Scholarly and detailed, yet a readable, moving presentation.

About the Authors

Kevin and Theresa Burke are the parents of five young children. They live in King of Prussia, Pennsylvania and are members of Our Mother of Sorrows Parish. Kevin is a licensed Clinical Social Worker and Theresa holds a Ph.D. in Counseling Psychology. Together they founded Rachel's Vineyard Ministries, an international outreach for men and women who have suffered the emotional and spiritual pain of abortion. Rachel's Vineyard is now a division of The American Life League.

Theresa Karminski Burke is the author of *Rachel's Vineyard—A Psychological and Spiritual Journey of Post Abortion Healing* (A Model for Groups—Alba House) and *Forbidden Grief—Understanding Post Abortion Trauma*. Theresa facilitates weekend retreats for post-abortion healing throughout the country. Nationally, she lectures on the subject of post-abortion trauma and healing, conducting seminars for diocesan programs and professionals.

Kevin has served as director of a crisis pregnancy shelter which provides housing, computer job training and programs for women in crisis pregnancy. Kevin and Theresa spent 15 years working in youth ministry. Together they established Covenant Family Resources, a licensed children and youth agency helping couples build families through adoption. They also work together in private practice doing individual, marriage and family counseling.

Author's Note

Rachel's Vineyard Ministries has become an international outreach to help women and men who have suffered the emotional and spiritual pain of abortion. It seeks to bring them to a reconciliation with God and their aborted children. We have come to see the words mentioned in the Introduction, "I will manifest my divinity," as an announcement of the powerful hand of Christ to heal and restore life. We are blessed to be called to this work.

We are witnesses to the hundreds of men and women whose lives have been transformed through the power and healing grace of Jesus. Over and over we have watched his mercy pouring itself out upon those in need. We have seen his mighty arm scatter pride and the obstacles blocking his love from reaching into deeply wounded souls. He has exalted the lowly, the broken-hearted, and those who mourn deeply. He has filled their hearts with hope and faith. We feel ourselves called to bring Jesus' great love and compassion to these women and men; his mercy reigns. He has reassured us of his presence through many signs and wonders; he has manifested his divinity.

We dedicate this booklet to all who have experienced, in any way, the pain of abortion. We pray that they may also discover the healing mercy and compassion which is extended to all through Christ's sacrifice on the cross.

For information on Rachel's Vineyard week-end retreats for healing after abortion, contact:

Rachel's Vineyard Ministries
P.O. Box 195
Bridgeport, PA 19405
Toll Free Hotline 1-877-HOPE 4 ME

Pauline

BOOKS & MEDIA

The Daughters of St. Paul operate book and media centers at the following addresses. Visit, call or write the one nearest you today, or find us on the World Wide Web, www.pauline.org

CALIFORNIA
3908 Sepulveda Blvd., Culver City, CA 90230; 310-397-8676
5945 Balboa Ave., San Diego, CA 92111; 619-565-9181
46 Geary Street, San Francisco, CA 94108; 415-781-5180

FLORIDA
145 S.W. 107th Ave., Miami, FL 33174; 305-559-6715

HAWAII
1143 Bishop Street, Honolulu, HI 96813; 808-521-2731

ILLINOIS
172 North Michigan Ave., Chicago, IL 60601; 312-346-4228

LOUISIANA
4403 Veterans Memorial Blvd., Metairie, LA 70006; 504-887-7631

MASSACHUSETTS
Rte. 1, 885 Providence Hwy., Dedham, MA 02026; 781-326-5385

MISSOURI
9804 Watson Rd., St. Louis, MO 63126; 314-965-3512

NEW JERSEY
561 U.S. Route 1, Wick Plaza, Edison, NJ 08817; 732-572-1200

NEW YORK
150 East 52nd Street, New York, NY 10022; 212-754-1110
78 Fort Place, Staten Island, NY 10301; 718-447-5071

OHIO
2105 Ontario Street (at Prospect Ave.), Cleveland, OH 44115; 216-621-9427

PENNSYLVANIA
9171-A Roosevelt Blvd., Philadelphia, PA 19114; 215-676-9494

SOUTH CAROLINA
243 King Street, Charleston, SC 29401; 843-577-0175

TENNESSEE
4811 Poplar Ave., Memphis, TN 38117 901-761-2987

TEXAS
114 Main Plaza, San Antonio, TX 78205; 210-224-8101

VIRGINIA
1025 King Street, Alexandria, VA 22314; 703-549-3806

CANADA
3022 Dufferin Street, Toronto, Ontario, Canada M6B 3T5; 416-781-9131
1155 Yonge Street, Toronto, Ontario, Canada M4T 1W2; 416-934-3440

¡Libros en español!